FINANCIAL FITNESS

FINANCIAL FITNESS

Exercises for a Healthier Wallet

B. VINCENT

QuantumQuill Press

CONTENTS

CHAPTER 1

Introduction

Most people are aware of the fact that in order to be healthy enough to live long, active, fuller lives, it is necessary to take care of their physical health. By paying attention to healthy habits such as healthy eating, exercise, and regular checkups, many people can prevent health problems or make them less severe. This module will discuss a few basic principles of how physical health can be converted into financial health. The same concept applies to financial fitness: by following some basic, healthy financial habits, the how-to's of personal finance, along with regular financial checkups, a large number of people from all walks of life can learn to control and improve their own personal finances. This means that they can afford an improved standard of living and financial security. Financial fitness is taking charge of your financial wealth by planning for short and long-term financial needs.

Many people in the US are confronting serious money problems that are not just the result of changes in the economy. At the end of a boom in which there were several years of significant economic growth, 1/5 of all households in the United States are experiencing economic distress. These families are having a difficult time affording the basic necessities that we all need. While there are people who may legitimately be poor for reasons that they cannot control, a large percentage of poor people in the United States would not be poor if they exercised more control over their wealth. The most important decision that people can make to improve their standard of living and financial wealth in order to avoid serious money problems in the future is the decision to take charge of their own personal finances.

CHAPTER 2

Part I: Understanding Your Financial Health

Exercise 5 delves further into positive budgeting strategies. It provides guidelines for tracking spending that will help you develop an accurate, insightful spending plan.

Exercise 4 introduces budgeting's purpose and describes how to measure and assess your budget. It also gives advice for making and living within a budget. After making your personal budget, review the healthy practices summary to help you compare and improve your budgeting skills.

Exercise 3 addresses common beliefs about wealth and net worth. It calculates net worth and encourages students to reflect on their personal definitions of wealth. After you finish your calculations, refer to the healthy practices summary for more information about calculating net worth, establishing positive net worth, and changing your financial beliefs.

Exercise 2 determines whether your financial practices are guided by positive principles. If not, read a summary of healthy financial habits to consider cultivating or improving.

Exercise 1: Your Goals and Indicators of Financial Health will help you clarify your own definitions of success, happiness, and well-being so that you can set real, meaningful financial goals. You will also identify four important indicators of financial health, which reveal both your current financial status and your progress over time.

The following topics make up the exercises: Part One introduces financial fitness, increases your awareness of financial health issues, describes dimensions of financial fitness, explains how healthy habits can prevent financial problems, and suggests how to establish a healthy financial future. This series of 12 exercises is an introduction to financial wellness, not an investment guide.

The quizzes provide an enjoyable way to check what you learned about a topic while summarizing the exercise content. They also offer advice and additional resources for gaining associating skills.

The following resources are available for your reference: Financial Fitness: Exercises for a Healthier Wallet offers a step-by-step path toward financial fitness. Use the exercises at your own pace to help you go from where you are to where you want to be. Once you complete a set of exercises, you can return to them in the future, whenever you feel the need for a little financial health tune-up.

2.1. Chapter 1: Assessing Your Current Financial Situation

By studying a business model, any household has a chance to follow suit. Firms make financial reports that shareholders can use to evaluate the business' health. But does the head of the household have any idea what the financial condition of his family really is? The problem with the average consumer is he fails to adequately assess his company's corporate conditions. Therefore there are a few basic areas businesses take the time to look at that each household should also scrutinize, that would include the balance sheet, the income statement as in how much you own and how much you have to borrow, as well as other categories.

Most people would perform as well on a financial report card as they would on a physical. The task could be daunting, but unlike our bodies, our financial health is possible to repair. A person's assessment can provide the necessary insights in order to complete the needed behavior adjustments. The focus for anyone in jeopardy is to bring down the deficit that defines their household today. In the business world, a company realizes it may be heading into disaster. If it can't dig itself out of the hole, bankruptcy may be in order. The company's options range from closing a particular division to dumping the whole firm.

2.2. Chapter 2: Setting Financial Goals

One thing Alden can do is to start engaging in exercises for her wallet. Using her fantasies about herself and the necessary education that she needs implies that Alden should become a really good saver, begin to repay some of the current loans, and develop good credit. However, she needs more specific goals than these general ones. Setting financial goals is a very important personal decision. Goals are specific assumptions about your future. They recognize the fact that you will need money at different times in your life to meet expenses and emergencies. Further, generating different assumptions about the present level of your earnings and education; marriage, the size of your family, and the standard of living you can afford; where you want to invest your money; and when and how much you wish to retire will lead to a variety of financial fitness regimes.

Alden is 26 years old and dreams of going to medical school. The only problem, though, is money. She has heard that tuition, books, housing, food, and entertainment costs are rising each year. In addition, she has been unable to save very much because she spends almost all she makes on her apartment, travel, and fabulous clothes. Alden has always been fascinated by medicine and knows that she really is interested in healing people. How can she continue her education when she does not have adequate savings?

CHAPTER 3

Part II: Building a Strong Foundation

Taking time to make a price comparison of some of your purchases now may seem like a time-consuming task, but may save you money. For example, did you know that the boot disk that comes with the newest software to download and install can sell for as little as $3,000 compared to thousands of dollars a month? Or that the exact same blood pressure medication can be priced at just twenty dollars?

Carefully consider all your print accounts. Are there any you can reduce or eliminate? If you have debt, try to identify at least some of the things you can reduce or eliminate. A combined cost approach is optimal. Comparison of prices

Write down everything you spend for a month. This means not just the big issues like rent, gas, and electric, but also a can of soda and an ice cream cone. You can also find a budget worksheet in the worksheet section. You can also estimate your expenses based on your past few months. Figure out where you can reduce

Track your expenses

How do you save money when you owe money to so many different places? Then there are regular living expenses just to stay at home and work? This guide provides some ways to identify and manage the money you spend every day.

Expenses

Follow the plan. Pay your bills on time to avoid late charges and possibly raise your interest rate. If possible, pay more than the minimum required. When you pay off a debt on your list, add that amount to another debt on your list.

Stick to the plan

Remember the list you created of your debt? Create a plan for reducing one of the balances one by one. You have identified some ideas in the earlier steps. Remember that debt is a cancer on your financial plan. You're squandering opportunities for the future if you are not reducing your debt and investing what you save.

Consider consolidating all your credit card debt onto one card. Different types of debt can have different investment consequences. For instance, interest paid on mortgage loans may be tax-deductible, allowing debt consolidation loans to better manage student loan or high-interest credit card debt. The presence of interest does not mean that you should aim to eliminate debt quickly. Before considering interest-only debt, consider the tax deductions and capital gains achieved on real estate investment. Create a plan to pay off your debt

Identify the balance, the interest rate, the minimum monthly payment, and due dates for all your debts. Sort the list, putting the highest interest rate debt first. If you don't know the interest rate on a debt, check your last statement or call the lender immediately. Consolidate your debt

Understand your debt

Especially when you are young and possibly supporting young children, buying a house, and handling any debt brought into marriage. Debt probably has a very tight grip on your wallet. Debt can feel especially burdensome for newlyweds. If your financial plan includes increasing your family, you will need to tighten and organize your belt.

Debt Management

Before you start a fitness plan, you need to do some prep work. The same theory holds true when you want to invest and plan for the future. The initial steps in financial planning involve managing today's income, expenses, and debt.

3.1. Chapter 3: Budgeting Basics

For some people, the word budget conjures up an image of penny-pinching and tight-fistedness. Worry not because it doesn't have to. By constructing a tailored personal spending plan, you can meet your bills and set aside savings as well as have some fun. After all, money is available to serve people, not the other way around. While a detailed budget cannot eliminate all financial difficulties, it will help you to make informed spending decisions and simply worry less about money. Being able to pay your bills on time, arriving at financial goals (e.g. a house or car), and having money set aside for emergencies or extra opportunities, means sleeping better at night. If your budget doesn't seem to be working, tweak it. A budget is not cast in stone; it can and should be adjusted. Instead of feeling that a budget is restraining, understand that it is useful and important. A budget will give you the freedom to make spending decisions with knowledge as opposed to worry.

Budgeting, also known as cash management, simply means making the most of your money. With a budget, you will know where your money is currently going and how much you have left to reach your spending goal. While this sounds simple, many people have never budgeted and do not realize that it really works. All too often people avoid budgeting because they think it involves a strict diet whereby they are unable to have a good time. This is simply not the case. Just like a diet needs to be balanced and flexible to be successful, a budget can also be flexible and tailored to your lifestyle. This chapter is devoted to tools and techniques for starting a budget and ways to stay on track.

3.2. Chapter 4: Saving Strategies

That is why it is so important for you to understand the concept of saving. When you receive your money, you should not spend it all. Even if you just save a penny, you are already training yourself for a secure future. Saving is also good because it provides money for your needs or future plans. They will allow you to pay for things in case of an emergency. Saving is about putting a part of your money away until you really need it. When you save, remember to always get a receipt from the bank. Got it? So, let's learn some more. There's no use in saving without taking good care of your current money. Money just doesn't appear by using a magic wand. You have to earn it through hard work. You should consider your savings as an effort to build an investment fund with your own sweat. Do you understand now? Now pay attention to the possibilities of saving money you already have in your wallet or that isn't already applied elsewhere. Just a second! We need to talk about one thing before!

Now we will talk about a new aspect of money known as savings. You should save part of your money, so that it will be there whenever you need it. What happens if you don't save, and you want to do something, or you don't have money to spend? You bring problems to yourself, and it really stinks, you know? Suddenly it looks like you're losing everybody because they can't understand your needs. It is really uncomfortable to feel that you can't get along because you don't have money. Only money can make you strong about doing things, going to places, or just buying what you wish.

CHAPTER 4

Part III: Investing in Your Future

Investing with Long-Term Goals Both IRAs and 401(k)s make for two smart savings opportunities for long-term goals. A Traditional IRA allows you to grow, tax-deferred, your savings until they are withdrawn. A Roth IRA grows tax-free. While contributions to a 401(k) are not taxed, the total amount you withdraw will be when you receive them as your income after age 59-1/2. Educate yourself on where to best put your money. CDs are insurance-backed investments at banks and often have higher interest than savings. Unlike other types of IRAs or 401(k), they have a fixed investment term.

Introduction Investing doesn't exclusively mean stocks. Often, especially if you're looking for long-term plans, things like a 401(k), Roth IRA, or CDs are better. Even if you end up not needing it in the long run, financial advisers will help you create good financial plans for your future. When planning for a long-term investment, remember the adage: don't put all your eggs in one basket. Spreading your investments makes them less of a risk.

4.1. Chapter 5: Introduction to Investing

As important as investing is for families, it seems to be an even more important factor in the success of many businesses and the economic health of many nations. The success of our world economy is in great measure due to the investment of people who put money into industrial plants, inventions, etc. The impact that the invention of the telephone had on businesses, on people's ability to communicate with their families, and in shaping the world we live in today was phenomenal. The investment demanded the realization of this invention.

Investing is also very important for the average person. It is perhaps the most important asset they can develop. If our money does not earn 13%, the impact on plans of middle-income families such as buying a home, educating children, retiring, or helping children start their own lives can be significant.

What is investing? You have probably heard of the term "investment". It is used to describe everything from the sex of rice to new luxury cars, from business expansion to a college education. Investing is, in fact, a critical means for creating financial opportunities that serve people in many ways. Many of the things we aspire to today require that we become creditors and investors. If you desire higher education and you do not have the trust fund, you may need to become a creditor and apply for a college loan. If you want to have a carefree retirement, you may decide to invest and create in advance the resources you need for it. Therefore, investments are important components of the overall economy.

4.2. Chapter 6: Building a Diversified Portfolio

An "investment tracking" sheet included in the chapter contains a first example ("Who Are These People, Chapter 5: Saving and Investing") for a tracking sheet that can be followed during the course to monitor the performance of an equity mutual fund. Data for the tracking sheet, as well as numerous other investment examples, can be obtained daily from financial websites. Suggest that students evaluate their investments daily, since numerous awards are given to well-performing investors.

The chapter provides valuable resources that can help you convey the importance of investing and the benefits of developing a diversified investment program. Among the resources are references to personal financial education websites and mutual fund companies. They provide information about financial markets, investment fundamentals, retirement accounts and programs, and investment vehicles, especially funds.

- Describe the basic asset classes, such as stocks, bonds, and real estate. - Explain the importance of asset class diversification to a portfolio's risk and return. - Describe various ways to diversify within each asset class. - Evaluate the relative risks and potential returns of various types of asset classes.

The purpose of Chapter 6 is to enable your students to construct a diversified investment portfolio. By the end of this unit, college students should be able to:

CHAPTER 5

Part IV: Protecting Your Assets

The best plan of action is to have a level of insurance that you can live comfortably with, consistently complete the listed asset protection ideas, and pray that you are fortunate to never need them. The most important thing is you don't want to do one protection measure and feel invincible. Let's say that you use a service to determine the states with the best asset protection for your future goals. You implement the plan for a few years and stop. You have a lawsuit filed against you in the same month litigation would not be allowed, and a judge sees you used the timing. They will not be happy with you. The secret to this section successfully is implementing the consistent use of insurance and protections for the best asset protection success.

If you've ever turned into one of those cartoon characters with dollar signs for eyes, you'll understand the importance of this section. People put a lot of time and effort into protecting their physical bodies, so the idea behind this section is to help you spend a little time protecting the importance of your financial assets. If you find yourself daydreaming about how you're going to deal with the arrival of at least $500 million, you've got to realize that all those dreams can disappear with one high-stakes lawsuit. The Lindsey Lohan and Paris Hilton's of the world understand the importance of placing assets where they cannot touch them—offshore!

5.1. Chapter 7: Insurance Essentials

Any discussion of personal finance must include a review of insurance. A primary requirement for sound financial management is the peace of mind that results from knowing that a health, accident, or other contingency that would otherwise be a financial catastrophe is at least partially insured against. If you do not have that fear, you have additional confidence to regard the loss of time or property as less serious in the face of adversity. The simplest insurance against those possible accidents, illnesses, or losses is a fund that is substantially separate from your savings but which should respond to you when required. The insurance company transfers to the insurance pool the realization of the disaster involved and personalizes it, taking over from the individual any chance of ruin and even out the loss over a group in order to achieve the benefits required.

5.2. Chapter 8: Estate Planning

Here's an almost absolutely sure-fire way for almost absolutely anyone to avoid probate 99.9% of the time: Nike, Nike, Nike. Read on for details of this whirlwind world tour to the land of trusto-nomics. Businesses grow, it is said, because of the wise selection of the rules under which they operate and the careful establishment of systems and procedures to assure that each business event has a predictable, profitable outcome. Because estate and trust planning is a specialized subset of business rules, it is freely available to everyone. All that is needed is the initiative to decide what the rules will be, establish them, and then see that they are observed.

There are several methods people use to avoid letting the government take more than its share of their estates. Some of them (such as life insurance and retirement accounts, for instance) avoid the problem by making your problems evaporate before you might arrange to take the trip yourself. But when you are gone, there are several ways to make certain that what's left of you goes where you want it to go. In addition, there are several other crucial estate planning documents that are critical to have in order to protect your property, final wishes, and your beneficiaries.

Being mortal and all, some long-term planning becomes necessary. When it comes to your estate, leaving decisions - and expenses - up to your grieving family (or to the government) is not the kind of legacy most of us hope to leave. Estate planning can be as simple or complex as your wallets and family trees allow, but simple and relatively painless (up-front) steps are within just about everyone's reach. For instance, regardless of age, at a minimum you should have a will to provide for the disposal and protection of your assets. And if you think you don't have enough assets to worry about, read on.

CHAPTER 6

Part V: Navigating Financial Challenges

Should you start getting behind in paying your bills and feel overwhelmed by your financial situation, stop and take stock to keep emotions at bay so that you can get out of the financial hole. Get guidance from a consumer credit counseling service. Most possess extensive information about debt management, as well as a variety of resources for different money problems. With assistance from a consumer credit counseling service, you'll have thorough budgeting and money management guidance, reducing or eliminating your credit card debts, receiving advice and information on bankruptcy, and possibly negotiating interest rates and payments with your lenders, enabling you to pay them back based on your financial situation.

At one time or another, we are all likely to face tough financial challenges. Should you encounter illness, job loss, or other setbacks, being proactive, exploring your options, and knowing your rights can help you weather the storm and stay out of financial deep water. Even though these challenges are stressful and emotional, it's important to keep a clear picture of your situation. Make sure all facts are in before you act. Research and discuss your options honestly and fully. If necessary, this is a time when you should seek sound, professional advice.

6.1. Chapter 9: Dealing with Debt

The key to being able to handle your outstanding obligations is communication. Start by communicating with yourself. Know the facts behind all your debts. What is the annual cost of each credit source? How is the current credit principal reducing future spending or investment options? Which debts are able to provide a tax break? What are the investment costs associated with continuing debt financing? In other words, what is the opportunity cost of spending in a credit-borrowing environment? Knowing the facts will often make it easier to confront level differences in spending behavior patterns. Avoiding answers, or not understanding your debt capability, comes at a high price in both financial and emotional terms. It is easy to become a slave to debt. But it is difficult to break the chains unless you are willing to confront the problem head-on, alone or better yet as a team. Openness is the critical element.

Understanding your debt is an important element in the course toward financial wellness. What is your debt capacity, and how does it compare to others? How is your ability to handle a crisis, and how should you deal with known debts creating a potential drag on your resources, your investment choices, and your ultimate comfort and security? These are tough questions to contemplate and answer, but we believe they must be addressed honestly and openly.

6.2. Chapter 10: Overcoming Financial Obstacles

Set short- and long-term financial goals. The essential foundation for achieving financial fitness is to establish realistic and achievable short- and long-term financial goals. Determine your financial fitness level and put yourself on the road to financial health. Manage your money to achieve important financial benefits. Spend wisely on essentials and perks to enjoy life more now and in the future. Juggle credit choices to maintain a good reputation. Save and invest to grow because financial fitness for life is achieved by growing your coffee can.

A vital aspect of achieving and maintaining financial fitness is to develop and maintain the ability to recognize and remove roadblocks that prevent or hinder financial progress. There are no huge steps in overcoming financial obstacles, merely the act of a series of small, daily steps of key money-management behaviors. By removing barriers to success and implementing changes to spend, save, and invest more wisely, you will accelerate the time it takes to achieve your financial goals while improving your overall financial condition throughout your entire life.

CHAPTER 7

Conclusion

The journey to financial fitness, like the daily commitment to physical fitness, does not end. Once you've achieved the ultimate body, it still requires work to maintain it. Just like the level of financial success you reach by following this thirty-stop plan, keeping this new lifestyle requires continual attention. Success is in knowing your habits and pre-empting mistakes accordingly. And, above all, motivation leads to results.

By now you should know what the fitness of your finances looks like and how much further you need to go before you reach your ultimate financial goals. You should see that there are exercises for every muscle group and beginnings of strength training regardless of your current condition. The final thirty stops are a slight departure from the exercises that you've been working through, because experts are invaluable when you need them. The majority of us would love to turn over the specifics of our exercise and diet plans with a professional, so please, respect your financial fitness in the same way. Seek out the help of an expert who can answer your personal questions: an accountant and a financial planner according to your needs.

CHAPTER 8

Appendix: Resources for Further Learning

- CARD (Consumers for Auto Reliability and Safety) - Consumer WebRatings - Consumer Reports - Electronic Privacy Information Center - Federal Trade Commission: Consumer Information & Publications, Identity Theft - Finances and Taxes After Loss (Federal Emergency Management Agency) - Insurance Claims Page - Secret Scores: How Employers Use Credit Reports - Privacy Rights Clearinghouse - Narashima, Dora L. Personal Injuries and Consumer Rights: How to Date a Shark without getting bitten. Atlas Books, available from 1-800-234-3733. - Outstanding Consumer & Financial Books & Pamphlets - Service Contracts for Home & Auto Repair - Warranty Problems & Service Contracts

Consumer Rights Issues:

Recommended web sites and books for further information on topics covered in this brochure. Remember these sources are for informational or training purposes only, and they do not suggest or imply what specific course of action an individual should take. Information at these web sites might become outdated, and any suggestions are not endorsed by the federal government. Please verify specifics with the appropriate experts or resources.